MW01294971

Narcissism In a Nutshell

13 Surefire Signs That the Person You Love Is an Emotional Manipulator

Zari Ballard

Also by Zari Ballard:

When Love is a Lie
(Narcissistic Partners & the Pathological Relationship Agenda)

Stop Spinning, Start Breathing
(A Codependency Workbook for Narcissist Abuse Recovery)

Narcissist Free:
(The Survival Guide for the No Contact Break-Up)

When Evil Is a Pretty Face:
(Narcissistic Females & the Pathological Relationship Agenda)

ISBN-13: 978-1539661634
ISBN-10: 1539661636

Table of Contents

A Note to Readers:

I understand that narcissism is NOT gender specific. Subsequently, in my books, when I refer to narcissists as being of the male gender, understand that, because I speak in great detail about my own relationship experience, it is for convenience sake only.

Certainly, narcissists do not exist only as boyfriends and husbands. They can, in fact, be male or female and come disguised as wives, girlfriends, mothers, fathers, sisters, brothers, sons, daughters, bosses, and co-workers. Whether the narcissist is male or female, all issues from the victim's perspective are equally important and just as distressing.

That being said, *Narcissism In a Nutshell* is dedicated to any **woman or man** in a committed relationship who suspects they are being emotionally manipulated by a narcissist or sociopath. It's a quick study guide to narcissism in relationships that should leave no question in your mind as to what you may be dealing with.

Thank you for reading.....

With love & sincerity,
Zari

Introduction:
Connecting the Dots

Although I've written several detailed books about narcissism in relationships, I've come to realize that there are those who want nothing more than a quick answer to that one nagging question: *is he or isn't he?* Based on my correspondence and conversations with narcissist abuse victims worldwide, this is, indeed, the question of the hour and, therefore, it must be answered. So it is for those who ask that I have created this quick study guide to narcissism in relationships. If your guy (or girl) is a narcissist, this book will validate that fact. After all, it's all about connecting the dots from one behavior to another. Yes, it's really that fucking simple and I'm going to show you how to do it.

As you will come to learn, when we're involved with narcissists, our lives become all but interchangeable. My story is your story is her story is his story. It's my belief that the thirteen "signs" or behaviors of narcissism that you'll find in this book are absolutely undeniable. If your partner subscribes to one, he or she subscribes to *all* of them in *some* way. All narcissistic behaviors connect together to bring us the inevitable "a-ha" moment. Trying to rationalize that that your guy or girl is somehow excluded from the label because he or she displays only one behavior or some more than others only creates false hope. A narcissist is a narcissist and if the person that you love subscribes to one behavior that I describe here, you will, if you choose to stay in the relationship, inevitably be subjected to ALL of the behaviors in some way, shape, or form. I guarantee it.

To be fair, while there's a fine line between a person who is a narcissist and a person who's just an asshole, the point is that there *is* a line. A person can be overwhelmingly selfish and arrogant, have a tendency to ghost after the second date, and even be a cheater and *still* not be narcissist. It's the covert underlying operation of the narcissist and that little bit of extra evil that makes the difference. In other words, when it comes to narcissism, it is the *level* of the betrayal that separates the men from the boys and the women from the girls. The bottom line is that an asshole can potentially be fixed and a narcissist *cannot*. Understanding this fact (and distinction) will ultimately help you to determine whether you should stay in a relationship that concerns you or if you should give the offending partner another chance to do better. Some people (i.e. a narcissist) can simply *never* do better. Now, having said that, the fact that you are here looking for answers tells me that you probably already know the truth and simply need a bit of validation. I can give you that.

This quick study guide not only describes the thirteen most blatant characteristics of narcissism in a relationship, it also shows, very clearly, how all of the described behaviors seamlessly connect.

This is very important because - *together* – all of these behaviors form what I call the **narcissist's pathological relationship agenda** – an agenda by which the narcissist lives his life and by which you, if you choose to stay, will live *your* life as well. In other words, these behaviors do not stand alone and don't make the mistake of thinking that they do. If you try to bargain with logic, you will always lose, my friend.

Here's a nutshell version of how a narcissist's mind-boggling behaviors connect from one to the other: The love-bombing described in Chapter I evolves into the future-faking in Chapter III in the same way that the silent treatment described in Chapter VI is a direct result of the managing down of expectations explained in Chapter VIII in the same way that the pathological lying in Chapter II along with the Cell Phone Game of Chapter V, the triangulation revealed in Chapter X, and the projection of Chapter XIII is all part of the chaos creation described in Chapter XII! Together and combined, they enable the overall mindset that allows the narcissist to perpetuate – and get away with - the "love" juggling exposed in Chapter VII. And those are just a FEW of the many ways that we can connect the dots within this book.

Narcissism, unfortunately, has become an epidemic in today's social networking lifestyles. These sexual and emotional predators enjoy the challenge of online dating where they can wear their masks quite a bit longer and catch the very vulnerable. Learning to recognize the signs/behaviors of the narcissistic personality can prevent the abuse from ever happening to you at all OR it will give you the confidence to finally and permanently go "no contact" and exit the game.

Do you suspect that your partner is a narcissist? If so, this quick study guide to narcissism is going to let you know one way or another!

Chapter I:

The Love Bomber

Even though a narcissist's love bombing involves all those initial actions/behaviors that, normally, we might consider to be "too much too soon" or "too good to be true", somehow the spell is such that we suddenly throw logic out the window. The trick of the narcissist is that he creates a "soul mate effect", appearing to be everything we want by mirroring our best qualities back to us. Moreover, the narcissist will do it in such a way that we don't even know it's happening. This tactic ensures an intense connection quickly with a desired target and creates the illusion that we've found our soul mate!

When we're involved romantically with a narcissist, the relationship cycles repeatedly through three distinct and, inevitably, recognizable stages. These stages, in perfect order, are known as the Idolize, Devalue, and Discard phases of the relationship and, if the guy is a narcissist, they will occur in succession without fail over and over.

The initial stage – the Idolize phase - happens at the very beginning and it is during this phase that we are subjected to love-bombing, a tactic used by a narcissist to ensure a quick and intense connection with a desired target. Ironically, many of us would be quick to say that a guy who comes on strong initially is less than attractive but with the narcissist, this is not the case. Because he's an

N, he knows exactly what he's doing and he is very good at it. The narcissist knows how to come on strong in a very passive-aggressive manner – a clever combination of skills that serves him well on those specific targets that he views as having future potential.

During this love-bombing stage, the narcissist will use a variety of emotional manipulation tactics to hook, re-hook, and then string-along his unwitting – and often love struck - partner. One of the most effective of these tactics is one that I call *the soul mate effect.* Along with its sister manipulation tactic future faking **(See Chapter VII),** the *soul mate effect* makes up the stickiest portion of the narcissist's evil web. Both tactics are so important to love-bombing, in fact, that failing at one or the other could cause the narcissist's relationship agenda to cease up like a bad engine. For this reason, failing is simply not an option to a seasoned narcissist. If he fails, it's a good bet he's not a narcissist.

And, yes, I have to admit (and not proudly) that the soul mate effect was my downfall. Clearly exploiting the fact that we'd known each other for ten years *before* spending another thirteen as boyfriend and girlfriend, my ex would use this tactic to pull me back in after periodically letting me go. In other words, after blowing me off and obviously changing his mind, it was love-bombing all over again just to suck me back down the rabbit hole. You see, an emotional manipulator will typically love-bomb a target during the Idolize Phase to sink the hook and then re-use the tactic in lesser degrees whenever they need to magically reappear after a silent treatment.

In the beginning, just like all of you, I felt as if my ex and I were *meant* to be together. For the first few months, it was as if we shared the same fucking *brain*. We'd finish each others sentences, we liked the same music, we laughed at the same things, I loved his sense of humor and he flattered me at every opportunity. It was amazing! And then, of course, he referred to us as *soul mates* and BANG, I was a done deal. *Wow...could he be right? Are we soul mates? Of course we are!*

Love-bombing via the soul mate effect is particularly effective because it is so very personal. Not only do we fall for the lie, we actually deeply *believe* it as well. In fact, we believe it *so* much that later down the road, perhaps as a way to get him back or to prevent him from leaving, we will actually try to convince *him* of its importance. *Please don't leave me! We're soul mates!* Because we frequently confirm that the love-bombing indeed works, a narcissist simply puts just a slight spin on the original event, thus re-creating the effect upon every return as an easy relationship reset. During those return moments, for example, my ex's soul mate rhetoric might go something like, "You know, I think I'm addicted to you. What can I say? We're soul mates!" And if he *really* wanted to tug at my heartstrings, he'd refer to "our history together" which, for me, was a key phrase that either caused me to turn a blind eye or triggered immediate forgiveness.

The difference between the soul mate effect and future faking is that the soul mate effect occurs only at the initial love-bombing stage and at certain reset points to hook and then re-hook a target. With the soul mate effect already in place, future-faking, which involves the narcissist making promises and/or future plans that will never happen, is typically used to *keep* or *maintain* the hook. In essence, future-faking is an extension of the soul mate effect and each serves a very important purpose in the relationship agenda. While both strategies are obviously evil in that they are pre-meditated manipulations intended to fuck with a victim's head for completely deceptive and self-serving reasons, to understand the association is how we connect the dots.

The trigger-pull to all of this is how the narcissist behaves soon after creating the soul mate effect - and, mind you, it's not a matter of *if but when* it will happen. Sadly, the narcissist will 1) create chaos and disappear *the next day* after saying all these wonderful things without an ounce of shame, or 2) forget the plans made altogether and then look at you incredulously when you remind him, or 3) accuse you of putting pressure on him even though it was *he* who made the plans, or 4) accuse you of ruining his life the morning after an entire night spent of him calling you the best thing that ever happened...and it goes on and on. It's all a bunch of pathological word garbage that, in retrospect, means absolutely nothing but when it's happening, of course, it's a heart breaker.

The Idolize phase is for love-bombing the hell out of you, showering you with attention, friendship, camaraderie, romance, and all those things you've always wished for in a partner. The N will make you laugh until you cry and he'll tell you how different you are from anyone else he's ever been with. He'll mirror every good quality that you have until you find it absolutely *amazing* how many things you both have in common. The relationship itself will feel effortless in just a short period of time and your heart will feel light as a feather. He'll use the word "soul mate" to describe how he feels about you. You'll start a sentence and he'll miraculously finish it as if, as I said, you share the same brain. Finally, you'll have found a lover who is also your *best friend*…the romantic element we always dream about, right?

Understand that when the feeling of love is real, no one will ever have to say a word, let alone try to convince the other that it exists, and promises are rarely made and then broken. We must re-train our brain to recognize what is and isn't normal relationship behavior… and then never ever settle for anything less.

Chapter II:

The Pathological Liar

A narcissist is a pathological liar who will lie even when the truth is a better story. This means that he'll lie about which super market he shopped at, where he stopped for gas, the hours he worked and what days he has off. He'll lie about his past, his future, his family, and his exes. He'll lie about his intentions towards everything – big or small – and he'll tell you he loves you when he loves nothing at all.

The narcissist lies by making things up and also by leaving things out – and he/she does it all in amazing detail. There are those who think the N lies because he actually *believes* the lie but I disagree. I think that a narcissist lies because lying allows him to continually create an environment where he can always be giving himself props for *getting away* with something. After all, everything is *all about* what they can get away with and don't you ever forget it.

To a narcissist, lying - just like the faking of emotions - is means to an end. He'll lie so much about so many things that your head will spin. You become so fucking tired from sifting through his *word-garbage* for a speck of truth that you opt for the lesser of two evils - believing the lie. Sure, it's the easy way out and exactly what the narcissistic partner wants but the alternative – to sit in angst wondering, worrying, and waiting - is even worse.

Narcissists and sociopaths live and breathe by a pathological relationship agenda and this agenda, of course, is all *about* The Lie. The narcissist will lie even when the truth is a better story and this is what becomes so maddening. My ex's talent for lying about everything blossomed right before my eyes over thirteen years. For example, to sharpen his skills, he would tell a little lie almost every day while, at the same time, deliberately leaving evidence of the truth – such as a store receipt – in plain view where I could find it. How crazy is that? Whatever I would find would almost always contradict what he had told me. And, because I naturally would address it, the gas-lighting (Chapter IV) and distraction reactions (Chapter IX) would commence, making the situation far worse than it needed to be. Why not *at least* try to pacify me by responding with "Oh did I say *that*? I meant *this*"? I would have been okay with that. Instead, the entire accusatory conversation became about the fact that I had looked at the receipt! A ludicrous as it was, he would continue the rant until I gave in, ending the conversation by profusely apologizing or simply growing quiet and giving up the fight. And thus, he would get away with it which, after all, was the original intention.

It's all a bunch of word garbage! Sure, we're talking little lies here but a narcissist's little lies are many - and they're all perpetrated intentionally to make you question everything. When we feed into this nonsense, what are we really hoping *to find*? The truth? We already *know* the truth yet we become hell bent on hearing it from *them* as if, by some miracle, that would ever happen. Why the hell do we put up with that? And how the hell does *he* keep getting away with it? He gets away with it by slowly training us – his puppet - to get tired of calling him out on every little thing. Again, this lying-related puppet training – also referred to *managing down our expectations* (**Chapter VIII**) – is all connected. So, *connect the dots.*

Long ago, I determined that for a narcissist to tell a white lie just here and there and only when absolutely necessary is illogical because they are *always up to no good* and, therefore, it's necessary to lie all the time. In a narcissist's mind, the decision to lie as much as possible is a no-brainer because it eliminates the possibility of him having to think too hard about lying about any specific thing. Little lies about little things creates plausible deniability every day, all day, and only by practicing his skills are all bases clearly covered. Sure, he might be *slightly* concerned about getting caught but the truth is that he's only concerned about the inconvenience it may cause for those first five or ten minutes just prior to him having to concoct a *second* lie to make up for the mediocrity of the first. The fact that these lies and behaviors have the potential to cause great pain and suffering to the people around him doesn't even enter into the equation.

So, the joke often told on narcissist recovery sites *"How do you know a narcissist is lying? Because his mouth his open!"* is about as true of a statement as anyone can make about this type of personality. Everything he does, everything he says, all those ludicrous narcissistic behaviors that we ignore…all of that is based on the premise that he is, by choice, a pathological liar. Consequently, we can, if *we* so choose, spin ourselves silly trying to unscramble the narcissist's mixed messages but it won't give us anything better than what we've already got. In other words, it will never get better than the bad that we have already have!

Chapter III:

The Future Faker

The N appears to be completely incapable of keeping any plans he happens to make with you but that doesn't stop him from making them! In fact, he only makes these plans to give the illusion that he plans to be around awhile. In essence, the narcissist fakes a future with you for no other reason than to get what he wants this minute and to string you along until he leaves again.

Aside from being the polished pathological liar about all the little things, the narcissist is also very good at lying about the big things and he does this using a tactic known as *future-faking*. By this, I mean that the narcissist talks about or hints at a future *together* to get what he wants from us *right now*. It's the type of narcissistic tactic that cuts us to the core because, like the initial love-bombing, it is so very personal. Again, we want to *believe* that these wonderful plans are really going to happen...that the person we love who is making these plans with us is telling the truth. I mean, who wouldn't? If you think about it, it's the *depth and breadth* of the lie that we become tethered to because it speaks to our heart's desires...*to what we've wanted all along*. The narcissist, of course, knows this and thus uses the power of faking our heartfelt desires to string us along until the end of time. It's the part of the narcissist's relationship agenda that lends itself to the fact that there is no boundary that a narcissist will not cross to get what he wants in the moment that he wants it.

Now, mind you, what I'm talking about here goes far beyond the periodic broken promise because a periodic broken promise can be easily forgiven when followed by a promise kept. I'm not talking about that. I'm talking about the *perpetual* broken promise that carries the allusion of a promised *future*. It's these types of broken promises that hurt the most because the lie itself is intensified by the authenticity of the way it's presented. The narcissistic lover will spin us a future via promises containing all the words we want to hear. They'll spin us a future via mirroring back to us all the things that we want from the relationship. They get us to stay or to come back or to wait for *them* to come back by *faking* a future with us that ultimately never happens. Future-faking is so much worse than ordinary lying because it shows how much of **a** pretender extraordinaire the narcissist really is and how far he'll go to hurt us.

For the first few years of my 13-year relationship, I made it *so easy* for my ex-boyfriend to future fake that all he had to do was allude to doing something together in the "future" and I'd ride that fucking wave of hope right up to the shoreline (where he'd gleefully slap me off my surfboard). Yup, future faking usually got him what he wanted which was to typically to stroll back in after several weeks of silence with little or no repercussions or questions asked. He simply had no problem saying whatever it took to get the job done. Even though I eventually grew combative whenever he even *mentioned* a future event (because I knew it would never happen), this didn't stop him from future-faking because deliberately deceiving me was... well... just too much fun!

Here are some of the twisted ways that a narcissist will future-fake during the course of a relationship just to keep us in his queue of his narcissistic supply:

1. **Future-faking during the idolize/love-bombing phase** to make us think that this person really wants the same things that we do in life. This type of future-faking creates what I call the ***soul mate effect***. Example: *"Oh My God, that's my favorite band too! Look, they're coming in 4 months. I'll get us some tickets – that's a date!"* or *"You know, from the moment I saw you, I just KNEW we'd be together for a really long time"* or *"I can't believe we like ALL the same things. I've never had that with anybody. YOU are the one for me."*

2. **Future-faking as a hoovering technique** but only when even he knows he's gone too far and we've had enough. Since, normally, a narcissist can usually lure us back with mere crumbs, future-faking is the emergency back-up in his bag of hoovering tricks. Example (by phone) *"No, no no...don't hang up! I wanna get married!"* or (by text) *"Hey it's me. Look, I'm sorry. Let's live together"* or (in person) *"Wait..look into my eyes. Can't you see how much I love you? I want to grow old together."*

3. **Future-faking to end a fight**. If, in the middle of a fight, the narcissist realizes he may be losing, he'll typically toss out some future-fakery to get you to relinquish control. Example: *"Okay, okay..look, can't we just stop this nonsense and get married or something?"*

4. **Future-faking as part of conversation**. Narcissists, as we know, thoroughly enjoy hearing the sound of their own voice and consequently will future fake just to keep the conversation going. Example: *"Hey, I've been thinking that you could really help me start my business. What do ya think? Wanna do it together?"* or *"Remember when we talked about France awhile back. I think it's time we started planning for that trip."*

5. **Future-faking as a form of gas-lighting (See Chapter IV...and connect the dots!).** Sometimes a narcissist will even mention his future faking as a way to make YOU feel guilty about something HE did. For example, in the middle of a fight or even casual conversation, he might say: *"I'm always trying to plan things for us but something always messes it up. You like to pretend it's my fault but it's not. I just want to be a normal couple ."*

Future-faking is used to get money or to recruit business partners. Future faking has been known to involve wedding plans or promises of wedding plans. Future-faking can involve lies and promises of all sizes and it's beyond our comprehension that such promises or plans are actually made for sole purpose of breaking them. But this is what a narcissist does and *nothing* about this behavior is acceptable. There *are* people in the world who mean what they say and say what they mean...but the narcissist that we know is *not* one of them.

Chapter IV:

The Gas-Lighter

A narcissist has a way of making us feel that we are going off the rails 24/7. What we don't understand is that his ability to make us crazy is an intentional control tactic. By saying one thing and doing another, the narcissist is able to keep us constantly guessing at possible outcomes and reacting to our own imagination. It's the perfect way to make a seemingly sane individual act out in ways that he/she has never acted out before.

One tactic that a narcissist uses to manipulate and create our reality is called gas-lighting. When a narcissist gas-lights us, he is either deflecting and/or projecting his bad behavior onto us or he is making us doubt the facts of his indiscretions even as they stand before us. Gas-lighting is the very fabric...the foundation...of the psychological warfare that the narcissist subjects us to day in and day out. Gas-lighting can also be extremely passive-aggressive so that we are often unaware that it's even occurring until way past turn-back time.

It is the narcissist's uncanny ability to impersonate emotions that initially gets the gas-light ball rolling. Especially in the beginning, we typically have no reason to believe that what we are experiencing isn't real....that all the wonderful things that the narcissist says isn't true. It never occurs to us that what lies ahead is going to be very dark indeed. Our tendency – especially if we're attracted to this person – is to believe the narcissist's pathological lies. Why? Because it's part of human nature to *want* to believe. Narcissists know this because they have carefully observed the way the world works. They understand that humans are basically *driven* by their emotions – especially in romantic situations. The narcissist uses this knowledge throughout the relationship, building you up and breaking you down over and over until you become nothing *but* emotion. And then he'll hate you for being *too* emotional. The narcissist is a gas-lighter.

The narcissist's ability to gas-light (a.k.a. fuck with our heads) is how he gets to do whatever he wants behind our back without us ever really finding out. The narcissist is able to create just enough suspicion to keep us filled with anxiety while never really giving us any cold hard facts. Gas-lighting is all about creating uncertainty and making us doubt our gut feelings (which are *never* wrong, by the way). Whenever I attempted to call my ex out on a suspicious behavior, he'd defiantly say, "You can never prove that!" And he'd say it with the utmost confidence. In looking back, I can see that he never really *denied* anything…he simply stated that I couldn't *prove* it and that was that. He knew exactly how to keep me separated from whatever other world he was playing in. Even with the facts right in front of me, he could somehow create just enough plausible deniability that I'd doubt my own eyes. I'm sure that you remember plenty of times where you found yourself apologizing for the soul purpose of apologizing even though it was *he* (or she!) who had created the conflict. You may have even fallen to your knees sobbing, *begging* to be forgiven…..*for what?* For catching *him* in a lie? Oh yeah, been there, done that.

What we experience with a narcissistic partner is trickery at its best. To get us wrapped up, the narcissist puppeteer puts on his best face, becoming a Pretender Extraordinaire….molding and shaping the emotional environment of the relationship in such a way so that he can always be having his cake and eating it too. By gas-lighting us into doubting our deepest gut feelings, we are often left to feel that maybe we *are* the problem and that perhaps we *do* make mountains out of molehills. No matter what pile of evidence we confidently present about any given situation, the narcissist can make us feel – without skipping a beat - like a piece of shit for even presenting it.

A narcissist will gas-light us by saying one thing and doing another and then completely denying the whole thing. This tactic is constant and confusing and serves to get the narcissist out of almost any uncomfortable dilemma. To get back in our good graces after a discard, for example, a narcissist will go out of his way to future-fake (i.e. telling us what we want to hear), saying all those things we'd been praying he'd say the entire relationship and making all kinds of future plans that he has no intention of hanging around long enough to keep. Later, when you remind him of his own words and promises, he'll respond with nothing more than a blank stare as if he hasn't the slightest clue as to *what* the fuck you're talking about.

There's no argument…he'll just look at you. As a result, hurtful as it is, we decide it's easier to let it all go and just hold out hope for a better result next time. The narcissist, of course, gets to chalk another one up!

You see, the reason that a narcissist is so good at what he does because he does something that we quickly forget how to do after meeting him. He listens. From the first conversation, the narcissist begins to process our personal information, listening carefully to our words, drawing out of us the answers to all those questions that he uses to measure a target's long-term potential. And while he mentally takes notes, honing in on both our weaknesses and strengths and calculating the future reward of each, his charm distracts us. By the time he moves into the Devalue Stage, we're wound like a fucking top, feeling suspicious about his every word and action yet seemingly unable to dig up a shred of evidence. Like all narcissists, my ex savored this process. Slowly but surely, I transformed into the lunatic he had been cleverly creating and, ultimately, my craziness became his justification for everything he did. Thus, as a Discard approaches and the narcissist starts accusing and twisting, calling us delusional, we switch into desperation mode because we know, without a doubt, *exactly* what's going to happen. He will leave or disappear, he will hoover and return, and he will continue to use, abuse, and manipulate. We do in fact, become very in tune with the *pattern* of the phases and can predict what this person is going to do. The problem is that the narcissist keeps us *so busy* apologizing for nothing and dodging distractions that we *completely* miss something very important - that, amidst the narcissist's word garbage_is the missing link we need: the evidence!!!!

Chapter V:

The Cell Phone Ninja

The effective 21st Century narcissist is a Cell Phone Ninja! A cell phone is the narcissist's very own Mission Control for managing communications across multiple relationships and situations at the same time. It's always about being up to no good and not wanting you to contact him while he's with someone else or someone else to contact him while he's with you. All communication is only when he wants it.

Narcissists are absolute ninjas when it comes to playing the Cell Phone Game. A narcissist uses the cell phone as a tool, a prop...a *weapon*, in fact...to push his evil agenda and to bring sadness and anxiety upon his victims. My ex was a cell phone ninja extraordinaire and I repeatedly called him on it, prompting him to play the game with even more sinister intent. As the years passed and I caught on, I was able to predict his every move simply by watching how he interacted with his cell phone.

During one three year stretch, my ex changed his cell number no less than fifteen times. His amazing MO was to simply vanish while simultaneously letting his cell run out of minutes. The fact that suddenly (and for no apparent reason) I was simply cut off from all contact – sometimes for months - literally crushed my soul to the very core. Later, although he vehemently denied the connection, I became convinced that the number of times he cheated was directly related to the number of times he changed cell numbers. I can honestly say that his most effective means of driving me insane was triangulation by cell phone.

With the dime-a-dozen flip phones, my ex had a field day. He would smash them, hide them, lose them and all at very opportune moments, of course. The possibilities were endless! Some of his clever cell phone tactics included resurfacing after a silent treatment with a newly reactivated *old* number (from years before) and sometimes even the *old phone* to go with it. I assume the intention here was to ensure that a vaguely recognizable number popped up on the caller ID – and this always worked, I have to say. Either way he did it, I envisioned a big bag of disposable Kyoceras somewhere that he simply reached into whenever he needed to cut me off, cut someone else off, or come back to one or all of us when he was ready. Now, of course, he must certainly have a smart phone and it's not quite so easy to do this – but I bet he misses it!!

Do not ever be fooled.....the cell phone game is *always* a key component in a narcissist's pathological relationship agenda. A clever narcissist learns that he can use his cell phone not only as a tool for juggling multiple relationships but also for keeping one relationship from ever *really* finding out about the other. By mastering all of the phone features available to him, the narcissist moves seamlessly through life without the stress of multiple worlds colliding. He may even pretend that he isn't particularly attached to his phone at all simply to distract you from the fact that he's *obsessed* with it. For example, my ex would sometimes punish me for calling him out on his game by smashing his phone to bits (whereby implementing "no" communication) as if replacing it over and over was simply no big deal. And he loved to say, "I don't even know why I *have* a cell phone. You're the only one that calls me." Yeah, right...

Narcissists also like to "lose" their cell phones just long enough to do whatever it is they need to do behind you back...*Did you try to call me? Sorry, I couldn't find my phone.* Sometimes they'll choose to keep the phone but "lose" the charger, conveniently rendering the phone "dead" just long enough to do whatever it is their doing...*Did you try to call me? Sorry, I couldn't find my charger.* And it doesn't stop there because The Cell Phone Game always has another card to play....*Did you call me? I don't know why but the battery's going out...Did you try to call me? Sorry, my minutes ran out.*

Yes, I imagine that before the cell phone, the Narcissist and his cousins Sociopath and Psychopath had a much harder life. They may have actually had to face their victims and admit the truth. Now, the narcissist can hide behind a nasty text or no text at all. He can subject a victim to silent treatments in the blink of an eye and a push on the keypad. He will Idolize, Devalue, and Discard you using nothing but text messages. He can be on numerous dating sites and manage multiple profiles across cyberspace without breaking a sweat. And he gets to do it all from the comfort of his own phone!

Keep in mind that the N is as simple as he is complicated and nothing about him or his evil agenda is rocket science. Once you figure out his strategies and see them for exactly what they are…ridiculous, ludicrous bullshit that no one deserves to be subjected to, you will start to wonder why you ever let it get that far. You will begin to let go of the narcissist in your life. You will be able to go No Contact and regain your sanity.

Chapter VI:

The Silent Abuser

Lacking the capacity to be committed in a relationship, the narcissist will be unable to fake an emotion of love for a long period of time. Consequently, he will periodically disappear, invoking the demoralizing silent treatment. This will appear to happen out of the blue and it can be quite shocking to the recipient. He may stay away for three months or three days, returning only when he's ready and expecting no repercussions for his behavior.

Narcissists and the silent treatment go together like…well, like maybe bees and honey or peas and carrots or (better yet!) thunder and lightning or like any two things that can't be one without the other. Seriously, the silent treatment is the narcissist's ultimate tool for inflicting cruel and not-so-unusual punishments upon those that dare to call him out. Without fail, every dysfunctional story ever told – including my own – that describes a relationship involving a narcissistic partner includes numerous silent treatments. There's simply no way around it.

The silent treatment is also typically the one single behavior that finally forces a victim partner to start googling the bullshit which, in turn, inevitably leads to the "a-ha" moment that changes (and also explains) everything that we've been going thorough. For the first few years, I had absolutely no idea what was going on at the onset of each one. I simply couldn't wrap my head around it. In the very beginning, I thought my ex most surely must be dead for him to suddenly not be answering the door or phone. It never occurred to me that I was actually being punished for something until the day he finally swung open the door and announced, "You simply will NOT be ignored, will you?!" *Wait...did you just say that you were ignoring me???* I wanted to die. I was hurt beyond any hurt I had ever felt about pretty much anything.

After suffering through literally 100's of deliberately calculated silent treatments over almost 13 years, I sometimes still think I carry the emotional collateral damage of the experience. Only a complete creep uses the punishment of silence to hurt the people that care for him/her. And make no mistake about it, a silent treatment is nothing but *a break-up in disguise.* By not telling his partner *anything* and basically vanishing from sight, the narcissist, in effect, keeps the wheel of hope/codependency in motion so that the recipient of the punishment, never being quite sure whether the relationship is really over or not and, anxiously waits for his return. The narcissist, however, will, throughout the silence, consider the relationship *completely* over and, thus, will (continue to) cheat to his heart's content until he's ready to return to the original victim (whereby making a *new* victim out of his newest target). If there IS one thing you can be sure of when the narcissist returns, it's that somewhere out there some other girl or guy is getting the silent treatment from this same asshole. When it comes to the silent treatment, narcissists are nothing if not predictable.

When a victim is being subjected to silence, it's easy to minimize the experience while it's happening in order make ourselves feel better. I understand that *no one* really wants to *believe* that every single time a narcissist goes silent he is fucking someone else – but he is. This is why he shuts his phone off or allows your calls to go endlessly to voice mail, ignoring your distress or why he refuses to answer his door (even though you *know* he's inside) or why he stays away from home (where he knows you'll eventually show up). For me, me ex literally appeared to literally fall off the grid. Even though I realized the truth about the silences and agonized over his calculated efforts to erase me, I still waited for his return because it never really seemed over.

When the narcissist finally does reappear, it's typically with a completely ridiculous story to explain where he was. Yes, narcissists don't, as a rule, put a whole lot of thought into the stories that accompany the home-coming because he/she knows that, by the time that he returns, you're ready to believe anything. Part of being a narcissist means fully understanding the concept of *plausible deniability.* They also have an uncanny ability to know when you just might be feeling a little bit better and perhaps moving on. My ex had an amazing talent for this. Out of nowhere, just as I was beginning to feel better, I'd hear the familiar knock at the door or the "ding"
of the text message that would suck me back in. This narcissistic tactic is also referred to as "Just enough, just in time!" (***See Chapter VIII – connect the dots!***) which means that a narcissist reappears at

the perfect moment with just enough crumbs to get his foot back in the door and nothing more.

No one – and I mean *no one* – deserves to be erased as if they never existed after nary a fight or even a disagreement. And a narcissist needs not a single reason on earth to vanish...to bring you to your knees...to make you feel like nothing more than a piece of shit on his/her shoe. As a passive-aggressive means of controlling and manipulating a victim's reality, the silent treatment is a cruel (but unfortunately not unusual) punishment that must not be allowed. How easily we are manipulated into forgetting that normal people *just don't act that way*.

Understand that at any moment during a silent treatment, you have the power (and the right!) to say to no one but yourself "This is no longer a silent treatment. This is No Contact and I'm in control." Believe me, if your narcissist is silent, you two are broken up – do not be fooled! You can turn his bullshit around any fucking time you want and make it stick. You can choose to *never* allow him to reappear. You can make this vanishing act his last simply by not being there when he returns.

Chapter VII:

The "Love" Juggler

The N will cheat on you numerous times – of that you can be sure. If you catch him, he will dismiss your feelings, threaten to do it again to shut you up, or act as if you are making a big deal out of nothing. At the same time, he will accuse you of doing the very same thing. The trick is to pay careful attention to the narcissist's words and he will, like a child, tell you everything you need to know.

Even though a narcissist is a pathological liar, there *are* those moments where he/she offers snippets of truth amongst the lies. We, as victims, can actually get to that truth if we would only listen. Yup, that's right, if we *really* pay attention to the narcissist's word garbage, 95% of all of our suspicions about this person would be confirmed and we'd know all we needed to know about *exactly* what the narcissist is up to at any given moment. In other words, it's absolutely possible for you to read a narcissist in the same manner that he reads you and no one – especially the narcissist – will be the wiser.

Now, it took me quite a few years, but what I discovered was a subtle but sanity-saving flaw in the narcissist's façade...a crack in the mask, if you will. ...and, I have to admit, it was foolproof! You see, narcissists, despite their propensity for lying about *everything*, are like little children who can't help but give themselves away when they do something bad. It has little to do with confessing, of course, and everything to do with bragging, accusing, projecting, lying, and gas-lighting all combined.

For years, just like you, I made myself insane trying to quietly validate a nagging feeling that my boyfriend was always up to no good. This feeling was usually stirred by his seemingly uncanny ability to accuse *me* of the very thing I was thinking about accusing *him* of. In other words, as soon as I'd gathered the courage to confront him with a suspicion, he'd suddenly accuse me of the very same thing before I even spoke a word. *How the hell did he do that? Was he really reading my suspicious mind or was something else going on?* Then one day the light bulb went off. In a flash, I realized that he wasn't being intuitive at all. He was, in fact, unwittingly giving himself away by telling on himself in a big way and he'd been doing it for years. The slightest suspicion that I might be on to his shenanigans would prompt him to distract me by accusing me of the very same thing. I realized - finally - that if I stopped throwing fits when I recognized a lie or when he tossed out a ridiculous accusation…if I just sat back and really *listened* to what he was saying… I'd know EXACTLY what he was up to. So, I shut the fuck up.

In my book, *When Love Is a Lie*, I discuss the narcissist's accusatory distraction tactic in detail and I also recommend using it to get a handle on what the narcissist is up to. This is a golden opportunity to turn his ploy into your advantage. Either a narcissist will accuse his partner of the *very thing* that he is doing at any given time OR he will verbally project this behavior upon exes, friends, co-workers or whoever he happens to be gossiping about while engaging in casual conversation with *you*. Again, narcissists are like little children who can't help but tell on themselves. If we stop reacting and start listening, we'll have the answers.

1. **If he accuses you, out-of-the-blue, of cheating or suddenly begins acting insanely jealous, he's either cheating or getting ready to cheat.**
2. **If he accuses you of lying about something ridiculous, he's worried about you catching *him* in a lie that he told recently. Think back and you'll find it.**
3. **If he casually chit-chats about a girl – *any* girl (supermarket checkout girl, co-worker, neighbor, etc.) - who "really gets on his nerves" or annoys him, you can safely assume he's getting ready to put the moves on her or he's already seeing her.**
4. **If he does something out of the ordinary, wears something out of the ordinary, or says something out of the ordinary, look deep into it. Quietly read between the lines and don't take it at face value. NOTHING a narcissist says or does is random even if he is not quite aware of this himself.**

I'm explaining this to you not because I think you should expend all kinds of energy reading the narcissist and guessing what he's up to but because I want you to STOP trying to validate your suspicions. You do not have to participate in the narcissist's game a single second longer. If you are still dealing with this person, I am giving you a great excuse to NOT become insane at his accusatory bullshit. I'm telling you that the truth has always been there. I'm telling you that this is a *foolproof* method for reading the narcissist.

Sure, the narcissist *appears* to be cleverly deceptive but the truth is that he/she is only as cleverly deceptive as the transparency of the bullshit. From now on, stop, look, and listen. Trust your gut feeling – always. Take the monster's ploy and turn it into your advantage. And then, with the truth by your side, do the right thing and go No Contact, once and for all. Do it for yourself and for the rest of your life.

Chapter VIII:

The Expectation Manager

Over time, a narcissist slowly **manages down our expectations** *of the relationship so that we expect less and less and he gets away with more. By putting forth only the most minimal efforts required to maintain his part, the N provides* **"just enough, just in time"** *to keep the farce moving forward and you will come to accept – and even beg for - these crumbs of attention.*

Think about this and you will see how true it is. After the Idolize Phase, the narcissist very systematically starts pulling back from all those cool things that he would do for you in the beginning. The initial love-bombing **(See Chapter 1...connect the dots!)** is performed only to hook you and then, slowly but surely, the narcissist must manage down your expectations so that you don't actually *expect* him to keep providing. We know this as the Devalue Stage – a stage where things begin to mysteriously go downhill and we don't know why. To the N, this stage is absolutely necessary. It is a means to an end and the core of the agenda. At this point, the narcissist knows that to deliberately expend *more effort than needed* would indicate a level of predictability and well-intention on his part that he would have to keep up – and this is not going to happen. So where the love bombing has raised your expectations, the narcissist must now manage them down to a controllable level. You will quickly learn that there are a variety of punishments for those who have expectations within the relationship.

What the narcissist does particularly well and with steadfast precision is steam line our expectations down to nothing so that we accept mere crumbs of attention. He'll do this very slowly over time with each silent treatment, broken promise, and other disappointing and crazy-making behaviors. Much of the behaviors are so passive-aggressive that we will barely notice it happening until it is well too late.

Take the silent treatment, for example. When we're involved with a narcissist, silences and disappearances will often become common place (**See Chapter VI**) and, indeed, this is the absolute best method for expectation management. My ex would disappear without a word – silence was his favorite punishment for all crimes, big or small. I would be absolutely beside myself and inconsolable while he was gone, often driving by his house at all hours of the night or driving aimlessly around town if I didn't have a clue where he was staying. Most of the time he would simply change is number, cutting off communication completely until he was read to reappear with a new phone number and new address. At that point, I'd be so relieved to see him that I barely asked him where he'd been, allowing him to just reset the relationship to the point before he left without repercussion. Talk about managing down my expectations! I would *beg* for the crumbs!

You see, for the narcissist, any energy he is forced to expend in order to hoover us back after a silence must, at some point, become nearly nothing or we become *worth* nothing. In the beginning, he may put out a slight effort but this will slowly fade away and it's all part of the hook. *Well, at least he came back to me. He must really love me!* This also goes for any other situation that occurs within the relationship where the narcissist might be expected to show up or pull his own weight or bear responsibility or be considerate or have your back. By ensuring that, eventually, the **crumbs of attention** needed to lure you back to the game are as low as they can go, he can basically do whatever he wants and we will let it slide if for nothing else than to keep the peace.

For a minute, imagine how the expectation factor works in a "normal relationship". When a "normal" partner *deliberately* expends more effort than needed in *any* part of the relationship (because he or she wants to), this is typically a healthy indication of well-intentioned predictability. In such cases, one partner, upon noticing the efforts of the other, will usually reciprocate the gesture while also "upping" his or her expectations of the relationship, thus keeping the happy momentum going. In a narcissist's world, this never happens. The N has *no intention* of living up to anyone's expectations (but his own, of course) so continually working to *manage down* the expectations of those around him eliminates the problem of ever having to work too hard at anything. It's quite a brilliant strategy actually.

Now, our own behaviors, during this devalue and expectation

management stage, will seem to take on a life of their own. Simultaneously, we may become both aggressive trying to figure out what is happening and submissive relevant to apologizing for things that are not even our fault. From his own experience of having done this many times throughout all of his relationships, the narcissist knows exactly what to expect from us and will even make allowances for our craziness as long as the end result is that we have no expectations.

The narcissist will use his management expertise to get us accustomed to many things such as expecting just the bare minimum (or nothing at all) relevant to birthday, anniversary, or Christmas gifts. We also become accustomed to his absence at all celebratory or family events as if it's normal behavior and it is not! In the case of emergencies, the narcissist – even if he is our lover or husband – may not be the first person we even call. I know that it was for me. At the end of my relationship, it was the absolute realization that there wasn't a single situation that I could think of – past or future – where my narcissistic boyfriend would ever *have my back*. And this was the "a-ha" moment that catapulted me to mentally breaking free.

Look, when we love someone unconditionally, it is natural to spend much of the relationship doing everything for this person and expecting nothing in return. Unfortunately, though, when we love a narcissist, *this is exactly what we get*. Nothing. In these cases, the word "unconditional" takes on an entirely new and nefarious meaning!

Never ever accept mere crumbs of attention. Never. In fact, always be wary of dwindling reciprocation on the part of *anyone* you happening to be spending time with – I don't care who it is! *You deserve so much more in this life....*

.

Chapter IX:

The Distracter

*Narcissists will never accept blame for anything that happens in a relationship. They will always blame the other person involved – you, his employers, his parents or siblings, co-workers, ex's, etc. When the threat of being confronted (real or perceived) is presented, a narcissist will use a distraction mechanism   narcissist is confronted with a lie, he will use a mechanism known as **plausible denial** – or, as I call it, a distraction reaction to deflect the blame back on whoever is doing the accusing.*

I really started thinking about this particular narcissistic maneuver after receiving a heart-breaking article comment from a woman who is going through hell right now and happened to stumble across my book. Her descriptions of her narcissistic husband's crazy-making behavior, the silent treatments, and her manipulation-induced reactions were a chilling reminder of how often I dealt with the same crap no matter how many facts I laid out before my ex. The standard response was always to deny, deny, deny or to completely ignore - and then distract from - the obvious truth by shifting the blame onto me somehow until he had me begging to be forgiven for everything I might have ever done wrong up until that point.

Plausible deniability is used as a narcissistic defense mechanism for automatically kicking back the insinuation that anything could *possibly* be wrong with him or that he would even *consider* doing whatever it is you're accusing him of doing. It matters not that evidence of his betrayal is front and center. Evidence and fact mean absolutely nothing. Evidence, in fact, will piss him off. The narcissist, in fact, will instantly deny that the evidence in hand is evidence at all. He will create just enough plausible deniability – doubts about his guilt and your sanity - that you will question the validity of your own proof.

The narcissist will, with mere words, distract you from whatever you call him out on by deflecting the blame back to you:

What are you talking about? You're delusional.

That's right..just keeping bring up the past!

Now you're just making shit up. I think you're bi-polar.

Now I know why nobody likes you.

I think you need to get professional help. You're paranoid.

What does that prove? Nothing! It means nothing!

I can't believe that you would even say that.

Oh…and let's not forget ***the silent stare*** with which we're all too familiar with (which says all of the above and more). Anything and everything becomes a distraction from the truth in the blink of an eye. Some, like my ex, will feign a sudden sickness (i.e.

migraine) or an fake emergency that he forget to tell me about (i.e. his mother had a stroke) or something *else* he needed to talk to me about. He would distract me with initiating sex in the middle of a fight...anything and everything to change the subject or flip it around on me so that I became confused as to what I was even confronting him about in the first place.

The words used by narcissistic partners appear so amazingly similar and universal because narcissism stems from an ideology that runs very deep...a *one-way* ideology that is at the very core of the pathological relationship agenda that I talk about in my books. Narcissism is basically a very covert operation and this is why we become super sleuths, always searching and investigating looking for the one big piece of proof that will finally set us free. The problem is that any proof that we do find is either not big enough for us or easily dissuaded by a narcissist's distraction. Even if we work our asses off to get the proof that we need, we typically don't have the slightest idea what to do with it!

We are easily distracted away from the truth because we really don't want to believe that *truth* is what it really is. As normal people, it is extremely hard for us to fathom thinking at the nefarious level that it always appears a narcissist is thinking and, therefore, we'll choose to, instead, "sort of" believe the lie. Sometimes the narcissist's lie is *so* ludicrous that it's even easier to "let it go" *in lieu of confronting him at all* lest we take the risk of stumbling around trying to get our words right. The N, of course, is hip to all of this and *counts* on our confusion – and his own propensity for lying (**See Chapter II…connect the dots!**) – to always be his free pass to do just about anything he pleases during the relationship and get away with it.

There comes a time when we simply have to be comfortable and confident in the truth that we know and *fuck* the proof. Our intuition is *always* right and if we paid attention to our gut feeling, we'd know everything we needed to know and the narcissist's distractions and intentions to deceive wouldn't mean a thing. Again, *we have to confidence in the truth that we know.*

Chapter X:

The Triangulator

Triangulation is a passive-aggressive manipulation tactic used by narcissists and sociopaths to instill feelings of jealousy and insecurity in their partners. It's a tactic by which narcissists can create thrilling illusions of popularity, making themselves out to be far busier and more socially-in-demand outside of the relationship than they really are. This narcissistic strategy, like all the others, slips quietly into the relationship over time so that you – the loving partner – barely know it's happening until you start to get "that feeling".

To provoke feelings of insecurity in a victim partner, a narcissist will use a tactic known as triangulation to create the illusion that he is far more popular and important than he really is. For the narcissist, the object of the game is to drive his partner to the brink of insanity over something that may or may not even be happening. By way of a passive-aggressive and very manufactured illusion, the narcissist will cause his partner to feel she has to compete for his affections with people, places, and things that she may or may not even know or that may or may not even exist!

If the narcissist is a proficient triangulator, he may even convince *himself* that he's more important and popular than he really is which, of course, gives an enormous boost to his already overblown ego. Moreover, if the triangulation is successful, *you* will find yourself acting completely out of character. Indeed, the creation of phantom competition in a relationship can turn a secure, confident person into a suspicious, jealous manic in no time flat. To add to the weirdness, the actual threat from this third part of the triangle, although intentionally added by the N, is usually something you can never prove because 1) he only alludes to the third person in random conversations, and 2) he looks at you as if you're absolutely crazy if you dare to call him out. Since the last thing we ever want to do is appear insanely jealous for no reason, often times we say nothing, choosing instead to stew about it quietly with a knot in our stomach.

Now that I understand triangulation, I can clearly that this tactic was one of my exes most effective ways to keep me anxious and insecure. There was always someone at work or at the bank or someone who happened to be a young friend of his mothers that gave me a queasy feeling. And to be clear, although narcissists are always cheaters, this third party is likely not even the person he's cheating with. Narcissists will triangulate you with one person to keep you *distracted* [**See Chapter IV...connect the dots!**] from suspecting the person he's *really* interested in or cheating on you with. Triangulation, as any good narcissist knows, always works better when the manufactured competition is random. This way, you're always guessing about how well they know each other, if this third party know who *you* are, or if the narcissist and the third party even know each other at all!

When the narcissist triangulates, victims often find themselves feeling jealous of people, places, and things that, under normal circumstances, wouldn't warrant a second glance. You'll start to question everything. If you've always known the narcissist to be a loner, triangulation makes it appear that you've been wrong all along. He obviously has *loads* of friends that you obviously aren't worthy of meeting! If the narcissist has always *had* supposed "friends", triangulation is used to milk his fraudulent popularity for all it's worth. Either way, the desired result is that you feel anxious, suspicious, and insecure about every little thing. You may even begin to feel guilty about your jealous thoughts and doubtful of your ability to act "normal". When and if you do confront the N about your suspicions, he'll call you delusional or needy or bi-polar and he will never admit to anything at all. He'll look at you with a blank stare and claim he doesn't have the slightest clue what you're talking about... *"Fine," he'll say, "I guess I can't tell you anything about anyone. All I'm trying to do is make conversation with you. You're so insecure."* And the triangulation will continue.

A narcissist will triangulate you with a girl, a guy, his mother or some other relative, a co-worker, a newly acquired acquaintance (that you will never meet), the landlord, a neighbor, the bartender, his boss...it goes on and on. The possibilities are endless. The sky's the limit! And this person he speaks of may not even be his next target...or maybe she is...you'll never know for sure. Narcissist *always* triangulate - even if you don't realize that they're doing it. Patient as always in the process to deceive you, the N will simply do it and do it and do it until you fucking *get it*...until he breaks you of all that confidence and security that made you attractive to him in the first place.

The thing that makes this tactic so amazing is it's extreme flexibility. In other words, triangulation can involve absolutely anything – even inanimate objects. My ex spent most our years together triangulating me with his cell phone...***his cell phone***! [**See Chapter V...connect the dots!**] At any given time, his phone was either glued to his hand, hunkered down in the pocket of his jeans, locked inside his car attached to the charger, mysteriously lost (when he was with me) and then mysteriously found (after he got home), conveniently "out of the area" and unable to get a signal, turned off, out of minutes, not working properly (until a call came in), on vibrate (so that I wouldn't hear it ring), suddenly unable to receive texts, or suddenly able to receive *only* texts. He always had a myriad of crazy-making excuses as to why I couldn't see it, hear it, know about it, or get within five feet of it. In my mind, that cell phone had long legs, cute hair, and a great ass. As a bonus gesture, my ex would, during a silent treatment, even change his number, making me insane. Whether or not his phone, at any given time, really *did* contain the numbers of random girlfriends, I never really knew...but he sure jumped through hoops to make me feel that it did. Sound familiar?

A narcissist will triangulate whenever he senses that you feel a little too comfortable in your own skin or (God forbid!) a little to relaxed within the relationship or when there's a change within his own life (just to keep you on your toes). For example, if he starts a new job, he may triangulate by casually mentioning – just one too many times – the bubbly receptionist and how much she reminds him of his ex or his sister or even *you*. He may let it slip oh-so-casually that he shared a secret with her in confidence that only you had known about or *worse*, he'll throw out this person's apparent opinion on a subject having to do with *you* in the middle of a fight as if it actually counted! The audacity!

Some narcissists, like my ex, will even set the stage *before* triangulation so that the inevitable betrayal will have the most impact. To do this, they may claim, at first, to actually *hate* the very female that later will quietly become the "confidante" OR they'll go for long periods not mentioning anyone at all and then - BANG - suddenly some person you never even heard about appears to be his best friend. Yes, the narcissist will intentionally *allow* us to develop *a* false sense of confidence and security *before* he smacks us back to reality.

Now, to be clear, it's completely normal for a couple to expect to share stories and have conversations about co-workers and friends...but nothing about *these* conversations are normal. Everything involving a narcissist has a slightly sinister edge to it. He can take a perfectly normal behavior - such as chatting amicably with a partner about casual events - and turn it upside down. It'll be the passive-aggressive way he slips his clues into conversations or it'll be the inflection in his voice or the attitude with which he says something. Above all else, it'll be the strange way that whatever he is saying or however he is saying it is *making you feel*. Triangulation is intended to make you doubt not only your importance in the narcissist's life but your importance in the world in general. It's a master tactic in the narcissist's pathological relationship agenda that is intended to *wreck* you and, over time, it usually does.

The bottom line is that a narcissist expects to be the center of attention at all times and have his every wish fulfilled by his partner. With each request that, for whatever reason, you cannot fulfill, the N feels perfectly justified in asking it of someone else – and specifically of someone whom you might feel threatened by. This is always the underlying threat. Triangulation explains the compulsion you feel to jump through any hoop necessary to please him even if doing so complicates other areas of your life. In the back of your mind, you always feel threatened in some strange – and often unexplainable – way by someone else in his life. Believe me when I tell you that your suspicions and gut feelings about this are spot-on.

Chapter XI:

The Holiday Houdini

A narcissist will always let us down – sometimes for the little things, sometimes for the big things, and always during the times that we need him/her the most. Narcissists are especially fond of ruining holidays, birthdays, and any type of celebratory event – particularly those that have nothing specifically to do with him (and even those that do).

Suffice it to say that if you're reading this book, you've likely suffered the heartache of being abandoned and/or rejected over the holiday season by the one person that we yearned to celebrate it with – our partner, the narcissist. Typically, this happens over and over again to the point that we don't even expect this person to be around much past October or November. It certainly was this way for me. My ex was the Grinch that stole my Christmas nearly every year for 13-years.

I won't repeat my entire story because ***When Love Is a Lie*** says it all but what I will say is that the memory of those Christmases past is vivid even today. The N was present, of course, for our first holiday season but that was only because we got together in October and he had no choice. After all, the Idolize, love-bombing phase must go on. But after that, my narcissist would disappear nearly every October and not return until – I kid you not – January 2ⁿᵈ. This isn't to say that he didn't *think* of me at Xmas. In 2010, ten days after I tearfully sent a Facebook message to the girl I suspected he was staying with, he was thoughtful enough to have me served with a temporary restraining order at 8:00pm Xmas Eve night. My suspicions, obviously, were confirmed. My heart, obviously, was shattered in a million pieces.

So, why do they do it? Why is every narcissist the Grinch who steals not only our hearts but our holidays as well? Christmas comes but once a year…you'd think that even a narcissist could manage to stick around or at least be pleasant for those few days before, during, and after but they can't. It's just not in their nature. With the possible exception of the very *first* Xmas of a relationship, the truth is that nothing and nobody is ever going to the narcissist into Santa. So, what *does* the narcissist do over the holidays, then, when he's not with us? And, if he *is* around for Xmas, why does he have to make it so miserable? I mean, what kind of person *plans* to ruin the holidays?! Although I can't, of course, presume to know what every narcissist is thinking at Xmas, I believe it must have something to do with at least one or some combination of the following:

- **He's a seasonal narcissist** – meaning that he spends his holidays with someone else every year. This is, of course, refers to the vanishing narcissist. *The Houdini of the Holidays.* The pattern and the length of time he's gone will always provide clues as to what he's up to. Because my N consistently vanished from October until after New Years each year, I wasn't stupid enough to think that he was *really* staying at his mom's during that time as he would insist. He'd turn off his phone and/or change his cell number AND sometimes even move out of wherever he was living. I mean, he *disappeared.* In the early years, I was able to find him, but later on and towards the end, I had no clue where he was at. I only had suspicions. Towards the end, it occurred to me that it was quite possible that – even after all those years "together" – I was actually *the other woman* the whole time. Talk about an "a-ha" moment! The bottom line is that if your narcissist is a Holiday Houdini, you can safely assume that he is NOT alone and that when he returns, someone else is getting the silent treatment.

- **It's too much responsibility.** No narcissist wants personal responsibility, least of all at Christmas time. If there are children around, all the more reason for him to run for the hills or become sullen – even if the kids are his. The festivity of the season is simply too much and, besides, *it's not all about him.* Even a narcissist knows that with certain celebratory events come certain expectations – expectations that he has no intention of filling. So, rather than wing it like a normal guy might , a narcissist would rather act like a dick so that *no one* has a good time OR remove himself from the situation completely. It matters not that your heart will be broken or that you'll have to explain his absence or surly demeanor to his/your children. A narcissist's only concern is that he be able to resurface after the holidays are over with no repercussions. He'll fully expect a post-Xmas pass for his bad behavior and then some hot post-Xmas make-up sex...and he usually gets what he wants.

- **It's not about him.** Narcissists keep us busy day in and day out with one crisis after another...and it's all about him. No matter what we're doing, he wants us to be thinking about him and it doesn't even have to be a positive thought. Negative thoughts work just fine and, in fact, actually work *better* because negative thoughts that go unresolved will always linger longer in our minds than happy thoughts. The holiday season, because it automatically causes us to focus on family and friends and gifts and parties and trees and children, is a source of angst for every narcissist on this planet. For this reason, he will start a fight, opt out on presents, give you the silent treatment, go to Xmas parties without you, triangulate you with everyone who might have been at those Xmas parties, and cause general suspicion until your brain is consumed with trying to figure out what the hell is going on. The narcissist's plan is that the effects of his holiday chaos will last until the season is well over and/or until all outside influences and commitments for *you* that are not about *him* have faded away.

The truth is that the narcissist is a *year-long* Grinch…he's the Grinch who steals birthdays and holidays and anything that takes the focus off of him. He is a celebratory buzz kill and he plans all year to be the best buzz kill he can be.

Chapter XII:

The Chaos Creator

The N appears to create chaos (out of nothing) day to day just to have an excuse to disappear or go silent when the mood strikes. Typical examples of narcissistic chaos would be the instigating of fights over trivial events, accusations of cheating that are completely unwarranted, nitpicking over every little thing until you snap, etc. Creating chaos is a deliberate tactic intended to keep us on the edge of our seats and in a heightened state of anxiety all the time.

Creating chaos is the narcissist's easiest way to control a partner and he will typically start the process immediately after the Idolize Phase to begin the devalue. Often the chaos created is so ridiculously hurtful that the loving partner (that's us!) will look the other way rather than feed into it and risk a full-scale war. The narcissist, of course, knows this and uses our detached reaction as his queue (and reason) to quietly escape. We learn quickly that he not only expects but *demands* that we tolerate his behaviors, cater to his every need, and always be available when it works for him. He, of course, never has to be available for you - ever. Moreover, if you dare to even question his unavailability or show a "negative" emotion towards a manipulative behavior, you will quickly experience a narcissistic punishment such as a silent treatment as a reminder of who has control.

The lover or partner with a narcissistic personality will create chaos and turmoil on a regular basis - and on purpose - to keep you in a heightened state of anxiety. He/she will do this even when things are good - and *especially* when things are good - so that you least expect the kick to the curb. This is why the silent treatment or a crazy accusation always appears to catch us off-guard, sending us into an emotional tail-spin trying to figure out what happened. Creating chaos is one of the oldest narcissistic tactics in the book (*next* to the silent treatment, of course) and it is absolutely intentional.

Everything that a narcissist does is performed for the sole purpose of keeping you on your toes, afraid of his next move, wondering what he's doing or not doing. Your constant fear that he's doing what you *imagine* he's doing (which, of course, he is) may evolve into super-sleuthing - DIY private investigating - as you continually try to prove yourself wrong or right. In our desperation to find answers, investigating will often become an obsession, making it impossible for us to focus on anything else. Considering the fact that we usually aren't even sure what we're looking for...now *that's* a recipe for emotional disaster! Again, this is all completely in line with the narcissist's pathological relationship agenda and, again, it is absolutely intentional.

This creation of narcissistic chaos is a passive-aggressive, manipulative type of behavior that ever so slowly becomes an everyday occurrence when we're involved with a narcissist. This chaos can take on many different forms and an emotional manipulator will adapt his technique to fit the recipient. The *point* of the behavior (s) is to compel us to *act* desperate and to *feel* worried and anxious. In fact, inducing these reactions is a very effective way of conditioning us to behave according to his/her pathological agenda. Narcissistic chaos might include instigating fights for no apparent , kissing you good-by and then not calling for days, accusing you of the very things that you're fairly certain *he's* doing, and other maddening behaviors. Creating passive-aggressive chaos is a powerful and effective way for an emotional manipulator to manage down our expectations of the relationship until we are willing to accept mere *crumbs* of attention.

A victim of this type of emotional abuse will always feel in a state of heightened anxiety. No longer feeling "safe" in the relationship, you may eventually have trouble focusing on jobs, children, friends, etc. It's a terrible way to feel and, more often than not, you may even be sure why you feel that way. The narcissist, on the other hand, will appear to be perfectly happy and will quickly accuse you of making mountains out of molehills.

Creating emotional chaos is all part of the narcissistic lover's passive-aggressive plan to control you. The chaos can be as loud as a fight or as quiet as a silent treatment and the devastating effect on you – the loving partner – will be exactly the same. Over time, you become an entirely different person and those around us find the changes not only noticeable but disturbing as well. Make no mistake

- our appearance to others is all part of the plan as well and the narcissist will inevitably use our seemingly erratic reactions as justification for describing us as psycho to others and also to justify his *own* behaviors. And around and around it goes.

The more you suffer, the more he knows you really care and the bigger rush he gets....

Chapter XIII:

The Great Pretender

Like a chameleon, a narcissist can be anyone he wants or needs to be in a second's notice. The N is an excellent people reader but, above all, he is a great pretender..a con man with such amazing talents that I have come to the conclusion that we're never going to know them right off the bat.

If the behaviors described in all previous chapters had to culminate somewhere, I suppose this very last chapter is as good a place as any. The truth is that we've been conned by The Great Pretender and this is the hardest of all the pills to swallow. To get to where we are at any point in the relationship, we have to know and accept that we were fooled in believing that this person was something he or she WAS NOT. We have to accept that the narcissist was an emotional pretender who faked whatever emotion was needed to get what he wanted from us at any given time. And we fell for it hook line and sinker until…well…until we didn't; until we went searching for answers and found them and had the awful "a-ha" moment. The Awakening to beat all awakenings. Yes, this person never loved us. He was pretending. He (or she) is a Great Pretender.

Think about the actions and words of the narcissist at the beginning of the relationship. ***Start connecting the dots from behavior to behavior***. During this love-bombing phase (Chapter I), the tactics of the narcissist are shrewd indeed. Typically, he/she will love-bomb the hell out of you, showering you with attention, friendship, camaraderie, romance, and all those things you've ever wished for in a partner. He'll make you laugh until you cry and he'll tell you how different you are from anyone else he's ever been with. He'll mirror every good quality that you have until you find it absolutely *amazing* how many things you both have in common. The relationship itself will feel effortless in just a short period of time and your heart will feel light as a feather. He'll use the word "soulmate" to describe how he feels about you. You'll start a sentence and he'll miraculously finish it as if you *share the same brain*. Finally, you have found a lover who is also your *best friend*...the romantic element we always dream about, right? Just like in the movies!

You see, narcissists can read people very well and this is how they do what they do. This is how they can be whatever they sense that you want them to be. My ex used to brag to me about this talent – about how he could figure a person out in five minutes. Over a 13-year period, I watched him use this talent to get what he wanted out of me, his parents, his friends, his co-workers, other girlfriends, and to hurt those that he didn't particularly care for. With each new circumstance, he was able to hone his skills until it became second nature. I'm sure he had been doing it his whole life.

The fact that a narcissist is a great pretender is the very reason why we shouldn't blame ourselves for falling for the ruse. In life, it's not abnormal to want to believe that a person that you find attractive and connect with is telling you the truth. After all, we're not mind readers nor are we supposed to be. Love isn't supposed to be a guessing game and narcissist's know this. They don't expect us to be suspicious of their every word in the beginning stages and so this is precisely the time when the ramp it up. Narcissists are so good at being everything we ever wanted and more that we illogically think we must surely be the exception to the "too good to be true" rule! How can you possibly blame yourself for feeling this way? Who *doesn't* want to be the exception? No one, that's who.

The difference between a narcissist who is too good to be true and a regular person who tries too hard or comes on too strong in the beginning is the fact that the narcissist can carry on the ruse for as long as he needs to secure his position. The regular person who is simply caught up in the moment right along with you will inevitably show a true color or suddenly be annoying or whatever it takes to snap you back to your senses. This usually happens pretty quickly so that nobody gets hurt and we can just walk away. This kind of scenario happens 1000's of times a day all over the planet and is completely normal. The narcissist, on the other hand, is wearing a mask that rarely slips until we're already hooked because it's held on intentionally. The narcissist intends to fool us and fool us he does. It's not our fault that he/she is a great pretender. It's simply *not our fault*.

Conclusion

As we move into recovery or as we struggle with No Contact or even as we suffer through a silent treatment, we mustn't spend so much time wondering *"How did I get here? How could I have fallen for this crap? I thought I was an intelligent person..."*. As human beings who long for love, although we might be *wary* of being fooled, the truth is that it isn't in our nature to anticipate that everyone we meet (and are attracted to) is an out-and-out con artist and pretender. This doesn't make us stupid or naïve or anything of the sort – but it can get us hurt (as we know) at least the first time around (and hopefully not the second). Our ***only*** means of protection – and I mean ONLY! – is to create relationship boundaries and deal-breakers and then commit to keeping and protecting them until the day we die.

With literally millions of narcissists walking the earth, the chances that we will meet one – and probably more - somewhere at some time in our life is fairly inevitable. Moreover, I've come to the conclusion that we may never really recognize them right off the bat. Our only hope is that we will get away quicker every time. While this is certainly inconvenient for those of us seeking to find a *real* soul mate someday, there's something to be said for knowing exactly what we're looking for and taking our time. We never have to settle for anything less than we deserve...and don't you ever forget that.

Go out into the world and be happy. YOU are perfect just the way that you are.

Speak to Zari

When we're involved with a narcissistic partner, only someone who has been there will ever understand what you're going through. Book a phone consultation with Zari and prepare for an amazing experience. Your empowerment is guaranteed and there simply is no more time to waste...

Book a consultation today at TheNarcissisticPersonality.com

About the Author

Zari Ballard is a home-based Freelance Writer/Author (and single mom!) who resides in sunny Tucson, Arizona at the base of the beautiful Catalina Mountains. In 2005, four years after her son's diagnosis with child-onset schizophrenia, Zari set aside the corporate rat race in lieu of a home-based career as a Freelance Writer. A leap of faith that could have gone either way, the choice was meant-to-be and she has never looked back.

Now, along with providing ghostwriting services to a handful of long-time clients, Zari plans to devote the remainder of 2016 and beyond to the world of self-publishing and to bringing awareness to her cause. A podcast series and internet radio show based on her widely popular blog as well as a book about her son's life and two fictional stories for Kindles are currently on the agenda. Be sure to stay tuned!

Visit Zari's blog: TheNarcissistPersonality.com

**If you enjoyed this book, please do submit a review
You are appreciated and thank you for reading!**

Made in the USA
San Bernardino, CA
02 December 2016